DK 24 HOURS
Water Hole

DK

LONDON, NEW YORK, MUNICH,
MELBOURNE, and DELHI

Written and edited by Zahavit Shalev
Senior designer Tory Gordon-Harris
Designer Sadie Thomas

DTP Designer Almudena Díaz
Picture researcher Sarah Pownell
Production Shivani Pandey
Jacket design Chris Drew
Jacket editor Carrie Love
Jacket copywriter Adam Powley

Publishing manager Susan Leonard
Managing art editor Clare Shedden

Consultant Ginger Mauney

With thanks to Lisa Magloff
for project development.

First published in Great Britain in 2005 by
Dorling Kindersley Limited
80 Strand, London WC2R 0RL

A Penguin Company

2 4 6 8 10 9 7 5 3

A CIP catalogue record for this book
is available from the British Library.

ISBN 1-4053-0819-2

Colour reproduction by Colourscan, Singapore
Printed and bound in China by L. Rex
Printing Co. Ltd.

Discover more at
www.dk.com

Welcome to the water hole,

6:00 am Dawn

9:00 am Morning

You may not know this, but during the course of the day, the creatures of the grasslands perform many of the same tasks as you. They eat, sleep, rest, play, and keep themselves clean. Visit the water hole and see how everyone from dung beetles to elephants spends 24 hours.

a life-giving oasis in a parched landscape.

1:00 pm Afternoon

6:00 pm Dusk

10:00 pm Night

Large floppy ears cool the elephant down by letting the heat of its body escape.

Having few leaves means this tree can keep much of its moisture safely in its roots.

In *24 Hours* Water Hole, we will follow a day and night in the lives of the creatures that live near the water hole. Over the course of the day we will return a number of times to the five animals on this page to see what they are doing.

Zebra

These horse-like creatures stay close to water and form stripey herds, so that predators cannot easily target individual animals.

Elephant

It takes a lot of food and water to keep an elephant going. The eldest herd member knows where the best supplies can be found.

Giraffe

Food is plentiful all year round for giraffes as no one else can reach the leaves they feed on. This means they can breed at any time so the males are always on the lookout for suitable females.

Scale Use these guides to help you work out the size of the creatures you meet. They are based on children of about 115 cm (3 ft 9 inches) tall.

Wet and dry seasons

8:02 am During the brief but spectacular wet season the lakes are brimming with water and a lush, green layer of vegetation covers the ground.

8:02 am For the vast majority of the year one or two water holes are the only source of water for miles around. The land dries out and cakes over.

Lion

With the king of beasts life moves rapidly between feast and famine. During lean times lions get skinnier and skinnier as they go for days without anything to eat or drink.

Hawk

Opportunistic birds, African harrier hawks hunt at the water hole, lurk in trees looking for eggs and chicks, and walk along the ground in search of insects and fruit to snack on.

5

1 Elephant

The chilly night is over, but the Sun hasn't come up yet. A troop of elephants gather round the water hole. Occasionally, in the dry season, they can drain a water hole in one sitting, leaving no water for anyone else.

The **lion** and **lioness** lap at the water's edge following a night spent hunting and feasting. After a drink they will doze the morning away.

The **zebras** and other herd animals drink once the predators have gone. They keep a look out for one another just in case anyone else is still hungry.

The **giraffes** take their time at the water hole, munching leaves – something they do for at least 12 hours a day – while they wait to drink.

The **African harrier hawk** returns to her nest hidden in a craggy rockface far from the water hole. Her chicks cheep urgently for food.

The **elephant** digs in the soil for salt, an important part of its diet. Young elephants learn where the salt is buried from older members of the herd.

Elephants live in herds made of females and their children. The oldest and most **knowledgeable** elephant is in charge. She could be as old as 60. Males **leave** the herd at about 13 years old and sometimes form their own **bachelor** herd.

Pregnancy in elephants lasts almost two years so babies don't come along that often.

The trunk is as useful to an elephant as your hands are to you.

Despite their **size** elephants are gentle...

Elephant skincare

If these elephants look a bit dusty that's because they are! After bathing, elephants suck dust into their trunks and then dump it all over their bodies. It acts as an insect repellent, and stops the sun damaging their skin.

Bathtime for a baby elephant

10:02 am This baby elephant is feeling a bit uncertain about getting into the water and dithers hesitantly at the water's edge...

10:03 am A caring motherly trunk reaches out. It first coaxes, and then gently pushes, the little elephant in.

10:25 am Once in the water all fears are forgotten. Adults and baby play contentedly in the cool water.

...but these springboks **scramble** out of the **way** when they approach!

Broad feet help to spread an elephant's weight so it's very steady on its feet.

The area surrounding the water hole is patterned with paths the elephants have created as they travel between the water hole and the forested areas where they go to eat leaves.

Insects and other creatures disturbed by the elephants' heavy tread are swiftly snapped up by waiting birds.

Elephants walk at a leisurely 5 km (3 miles) per hour, but they

Elephants can communicate with each other over distances as far as 2.5 km (1.5 miles). We can't hear these sounds, so it surprises us when many elephants suddenly arrive at the water hole at the same time.

can **run** at 40 km (25 miles)

Pooh!

Recycling elephant dung

8:10 am Unable to digest their food very efficiently, a lot of useful matter remains in the 100 kg (220 lbs) of dung produced by an **elephant** each day.

8:20 am First to arrive are **butterflies**. They cluster round the fresh dung and suck out the nutritious liquid.

10:00 am **Birds** eat the seeds contained in the dung, and pluck out undigested grass and straw to use in building their nests.

5:00 pm **Dung beetles** form the dung into small, compact balls. They determinedly roll these to their tunnels and lay eggs on them.

11:00 pm If what remains by now is damp enough, **mushrooms** may start to sprout from the dung pile. That means food for yet more animals.

There's safety in numbers for the members of a herd. If you're a strong healthy animal and a hungry lion appears while you're grazing, there's a good chance the unlucky victim will be someone else!

Most grazing animals drink at least once every day, so they can't stray far from the water hole. The tracks they make as they travel between feeding grounds and the water hole are etched into the landscape.

When food is scarce, male impalas have no energy to defend their territory or fight for females.

If attacked, this tranquil herd of impalas will **explode** into a chaotic frenzy of leaping to **confuse** their attackers.

Home on the plains

Peculiar-looking wildebeest wander over vast distances in search of grass and water.

8:00 am Zebras live in family groups. They graze together and groom one another by nibbling at each other's backs and manes.

8:35 am Two males rear up, kicking and biting each other. They are competing to head the group and breed with the females.

8:41 am Mothers are very close to their young. Relatively few zebra foals are killed by predators as the herd protects them well.

8:56 am Sensing danger, they scatter. Stripes make it harder for a predator to single out an individual.

9:00 am

1 Combretum tree   2 Giraffe
3 Guinea fowl   4 Zebra   5 Springbok

Mid-morning at the water hole and it's busy, but the animals queue patiently to wait their turn. Fights hardly ever break out because everyone knows the rules and makes way for the elephants.

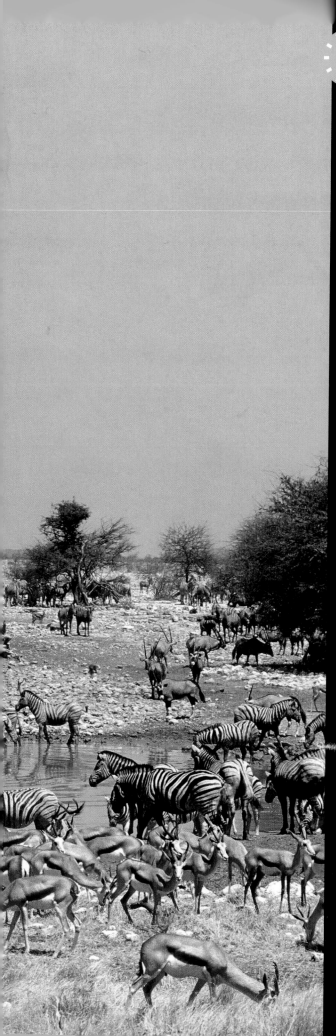

The lions are still relaxing. They don't have to be constantly alert because, at the top of the food chain, there is no one to prey on them.

The zebras are milling around near the water. Their stripey coats dazzle their enemies and may also help them cope with the extreme heat.

The giraffes interlock necks and struggle together but don't injure each other. This play-fighting between young males is called sparring.

In the branches of a tree the harrier hawk looks for food. As well as small animals, she will eat palm nut husks if she can find them.

Dust baths are a fun and important part of the elephant's routine. The dust gives the elephant its familiar dusty look.

There's plenty of high drama low down. Smaller predators like hyenas and jackals win their prey more with daring than with muscle, while rodents and insects spend time both above and below ground.

Bat-eared foxes listen for insects beneath the soil and then snap them up.

Dung beetles collect animal droppings and take them home as food.

Termites live in enormous underground colonies and eat dead and rotting matter.

The pack can take on and bring down a large animal like a

Cape ground squirrels live underground where it's quite chilly. They dig for roots and bulbs, and come up to the surface to sunbathe!

Spotted hyenas sometimes hunt alone but usually do better by co-operating and hunting in packs.

zebra or even a wildebeest.

Providing food for the family

10:29 am Black-backed jackals will eat most things. A jackal attacks a flock of sandgrouse by the water's edge, making them scatter.

10:33 am Having caught and killed a bird, the challenge is to avoid having this prize snatched away by bigger predators on the way home.

10:40 am Three hungry cubs are waiting for their share back at the den. In a few months time they too will be out hunting for food.

It's great being tall. Giraffes can reach the juicy leaves at the top of the tree and see hungry lions a long way off. But there's at least one big disadvantage – it's a long way down to get a drink.

Responsible drinking

11:02 am It's safe to drink so this giraffe starts to move its front legs apart.

18

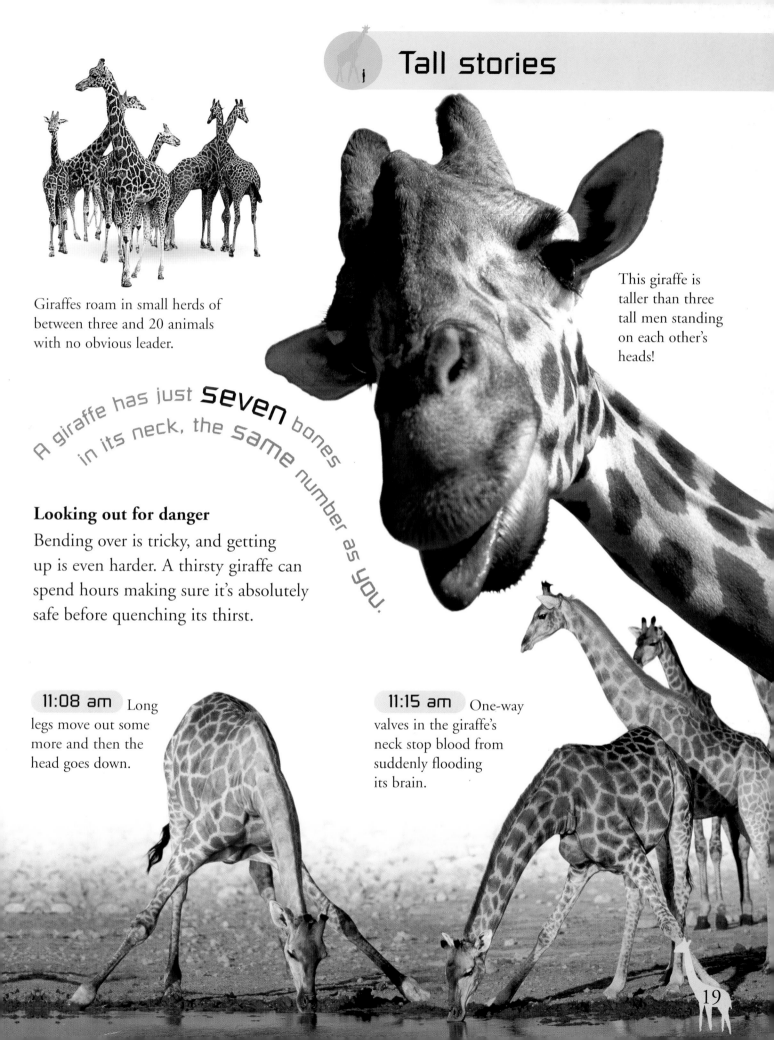

Giraffes roam in small herds of between three and 20 animals with no obvious leader.

This giraffe is taller than three tall men standing on each other's heads!

A giraffe has just **seven** bones in its neck, the same number as you.

Looking out for danger

Bending over is tricky, and getting up is even harder. A thirsty giraffe can spend hours making sure it's absolutely safe before quenching its thirst.

11:08 am Long legs move out some more and then the head goes down.

11:15 am One-way valves in the giraffe's neck stop blood from suddenly flooding its brain.

19

The birds that visit the water hole are extremely varied. They range from enormous ostriches to tiny oxpeckers, flesh-eating storks to insect-crunching hornbills, and group-loving guineafowl to solitary storks.

Delicate and pretty they may be, but **lilac-breasted rollers** make a surprisingly harsh squawking sound!

Oxpeckers and giraffes form an **unlikely** partnership. The little birds keep the giraffes free of **ticks** and **fleas**.

Oxpeckers have been known to take advantage of their host by keeping the giraffe's insect wounds open so they can feed on its blood.

Ostriches are the largest birds in the world. They don't need much water but they travel far in search of food even though they are unable to fly.

The beak is mostly hollow so it is not as heavy and bulky as it looks.

Perched on top of an anthill, a Marabou stork surveys the area. The thousands of ants living here have nothing to fear – the stork is only interested in eating meat.

This bush cricket's defence is the **stink** it gives off when attacked.

This **yellow-billed hornbill** uses its beak to grab and eat seeds and insects – including spiders and scorpions – from the ground.

Guineafowl live in large flocks. By day they peck at the ground in search of food. At dusk their cackle can be heard as they settle for the night

In many parts of the world people keep guineafowl so they can eat them.

21

1 Gemsbok   2 Springbok

It's the hottest time of the day, and the water hole resembles a swimming pool. Animals wade into the water and bathe, just passing the time till the temperature cools down.

What's up at 1 o'clock?

Lion cubs scramble over the **lioness** playfully. They are practising the skills they will use when they come to hunt as adults.

The **zebras** spend calm hours grazing at the dry, yellowish grass. Their diet consists almost entirely of grass with a few leaves and buds.

One of the **giraffes** crunches some bones. Giraffes have very tough mouths and tongues and like chewing on bones and thorns.

Soaring high above the water hole the **harrier hawk** seems to be tossed about by currents of air, but actually her flight is very stable.

The **elephant** plays in the water to keep cool. Its trunk can hold 10 litres (2.6 gallons) of water and is a powerful water pistol!

A **combretum** tree provides more than **shade** – its leaves, flowers, seeds, and roots are a baboon **banquet!** Baboons also eat whatever wanders by. Insects, birds, lizards, and small animals should beware if they don't want to become somebody's **lunch**.

The adults sit quietly – it is really too hot to be rushing around.

Babies catch a ride on their mothers' backs.

24

Young baboons playfully chase one another up the branches of a tree, and scamper around the trunk.

During a friendly grooming session, the baboon doing the grooming gets to eat all the **juicy** bugs it finds!

One of the gang

Being a baboon means doing everything together. Baboon gangs sleep in the same tree, and spend their days nearby looking for food, and drinking at the water hole.

During grooming, baboons lick each other. They love the salty taste.

25

The relatively few trees dotting the landscape have very deep roots that enable them to survive long periods with no rain. Their leaves and fruit provide food for a variety of insects, birds, and small animals.

Sociable weaver birds build enormous nests. Each bird has its own "apartment".

Black mambas can move as fast as you can run. And their venom is deadly.

26

About 40 baboons sleep at this baboon base camp and spend the day on the ground nearby.

Clever killers

Boomslangs climb trees and slither between branches to catch lizards and even birds. As they chew their prey they inject a lethal poison into it.

Skinks scuttle around looking for spiders and insects to eat. If attacked a skink can shed its tail in order to make a quick getaway.

This mother **scorpion** carries her babies on her back. Over time their exoskeletons (bony coverings) will gradually darken and harden.

Unusually for an owl, the **pearl-spotted owlet** often hunts by day. Despite its small size it is very strong and isn't afraid to attack prey bigger than itself.

Combretum trees can grow very large. Rhinos love to munch on the young leaves. As the tree grows older, deep cracks form in the bark, which will provide homes to many small creatures.

27

Warthogs normally live in burrows that have been dug by other animals.

The dusty earth looks uninviting, but many insects and reptiles find somewhere to live and a plentiful supply of food on or just below the ground. When the heat gets unbearable they sit it out under ground or in water and wait for cooler days.

Two pairs of bumpy "warts" between eyes and tusks give this peculiar-looking animal its name.

Impressive tusks are used for defence against lions and leopards. The lower set are very sharp.

Like their piggy cooling wallow

Wet and dry survival strategies

Bullfrogs live underground during very dry periods so as not to dry out.

The forked tongue of the **rock monitor lizard** has no taste buds, but it can detect nearby prey by picking up scent particles in the air.

Rhinoceros beetles can carry 100 times their own weight, which makes them the strongest animals on Earth.

During very dry weather, female **leopard tortoises** will urinate on the ground to make it soft enough to bury their eggs.

The most remarkable feature of the flap-necked chameleon is its tongue. The same length as the chameleon's body, it is spring-loaded and also fitted with a sucker. Needless to say, it is remarkably effective at snatching and gobbling up insects.

Terrapins are turtles that live in water. They start life eating insects, but later turn to underwater plants and seaweed.

relatives, warthogs **adore** a in a muddy pool.

27

Sun-loving

At sunrise the whole mob emerges from their chilly burrow to warm up!

meerkats live in vast **underground** dens. Each member of the **mob** has a job. Baby-sitters in the den watch over the little ones, sentries outside keep a lookout for **danger**, hunters find food, and teachers **train** young meerkats to hunt.

Co-operation is the name of the game in a meerkat mob. Hunters always bring their food home to share.

Look out!

Sentries cheep or cluck if they sense danger, and bark or growl more alarmingly if a hawk or jackal approaches. Everyone instantly dives for cover.

Meerkat munchies

Powerful front claws make digging up **beetles** a doddle!

Worms, along with beetles, spiders, and other bugs, are an important part of the meerkat diet.

Scorpions are gulped down before they can bite. Or perhaps meerkats are immune to venom.

At the **lookout post**, sentries perch on their hind legs, using their **tails** for balance.

Bolt-holes mean meerkats can make a swift exit if danger looms.

31

1 Leopard **2** Lion

Dusk descends quickly at the water hole. The large predators such as lions and leopards perk up as the temperature cools down. A pride of lions sharpen their claws on a convenient tree trunk.

The **lion** is the only adult male lion in the pride. He marks his territory with urine to warn other lions to stay out of his patch.

The **zebras** head for the clearing where they will spend the night. They won't go further than 12 km (7 miles) from the water hole.

This **giraffe** is still feeding on leaves as the sun sets. Male giraffes are taller than females so they don't compete for the same leaves.

Hovering under a sociable weavers' nest and using a leg to investigate, the **harrier hawk** looks for eggs or chicks to eat.

The **elephant's** trunk reaches out and expertly strips trees of leaves and branches. An incredible 50,000 muscles make it a very precise tool.

Roaring, not purring

Cheetahs are built for speed, not strength, so they don't always manage to keep their prey once they have caught it.

Caracals mostly eat birds and mice. They can spring as high as 3 m (10 ft) into the air to swipe and grab at birds as they fly past.

Lions are the most sociable of the big cats. They live in groups known as prides whose members co-operate by hunting together.

From its vantage point up a tree, a **leopard** quietly locates its victim and suddenly drops down for the kill.

Servals usually hunt at dusk, leaping up high and whacking their prey with their forepaws.

Most cats, with the exception of lions, live and hunt alone. They stalk their prey by silently creeping around close to the ground and then suddenly pouncing. Pinning their victim down, they strangle it, finishing the job with a lethal bite to the windpipe to cut off its breathing.

Cheetahs are the **fastest** animals on earth. They can run at 100 km (62 miles) per hour but only fo[

Once a leopard has caught its prey it drags it up a tree. A hungry leopard eats there, away from scavenging jackals and hyenas. If it's not hungry, the meat is hidden away for later.

20 seconds at a time.

The cheetah's long tail helps it to make sudden sharp turns while giving chase.

Cats' eyes work very well at night. Cats see as clearly by starlight as a human sees by daylight.

After a kill, lions gobble down their food and then spend a day or so on a long after-dinner doze. They can afford to do this because no other animal dares attack a lion, and anyway, it's a good way to pass the time between meals...

The job of the oldest male is to guard the pride.

The core of the pride are the 4-6 related lionesses who give birth at around the same time and look after each other's cubs.

Fresh meat for dinner

8:03 am After many hours in wait, a lioness selects her target – one of the weaker kudus in the herd.

8:04 am She runs powerfully towards her victim. Panicking, the kudu notices too late and tries to flee.

8:05 am The lioness grabs the kudu. With a swipe at the legs and a bite to the spine, this kudu stands no chance.

8:15 am Other lions join the hunter and tuck into a big meal. The next few hours will be spent digesting!

Yawnnnnn

When a lion yawns, rather than roars, you can see its enormous tongue. It is covered with hard bumps, rough enough to scrape meat from bones.

Lion cubs in the lair greet their mother excitedly on her return from a hunting trip. She leads them to her kill for a share of the meat.

Lions prefer fresh meat, but the leftovers don't just lie around decomposing. Scavengers polish them off. They'll eat anything that was once alive! As nature's rubbish collectors and recyclers they consume every last scrap of flesh and bone left by the big hunters.

The lion in the pride hangs back. He watches distance and then barges

Lionesses drink after a kill. Although they are the hunters and actually do all the hard work, the males of the pride usually eat first, followed by the lionesses, and then the cubs.

the **action** lazily from a

in to get the first bite!

This wildebeest will be just a skeleton within a few hours. Only a very hungry hyena would devour the bones.

Enough for everybody

9:14 pm High in the sky, **African white-backed vultures** use their amazing eyesight to spot the dead wildebeest far below. They make cackling and hissing sounds as they feast.

9:21 pm Hyenas arrive as the vultures leave. They bolt their food down, eating as much as a third of their own body weight, before sloping off across the plains.

9:25 pm Lappet-faced **vultures** scare the hyenas away. By ripping through the wildebeest's hide with their hooked beaks, they make it easier for other scavengers to feed next.

9:46 pm Black-backed **jackals** eat quickly, expecting to be pushed out of the way when larger scavengers arrive. Back in their den, they regurgitate some food for their young.

9:50 pm Marabou storks pick at the flesh of the wildebeest. They are bald so there are no feathers to get mucky when they poke their heads into the rotting carcass.

1 Rhinoceros   2 Giraffe

Late at night the rustling of the undergrowth signals the arrival of rhinos and giraffes. Many other large animals, including elephants and lions, also come to drink during the cool hours of darkness.

The **lions** tuck into an unfortunate impala. They eat as much as they can, as it may be another couple of days before their next kill.

The **zebras** huddle together at night. They lie down to sleep but there are always some members of the herd awake, alert for danger.

The **giraffes** look wide awake. They bend their heads back against their bodies and sleep deeply for just a few minutes each night.

The **harrier hawk** spends some of the night in her nest, but also goes out hunting when her unsuspecting prey is resting.

The **elephant** needs around 200 litres (53 gallons) of water every day. To get its fill, the elephant spends much of the night drinking.

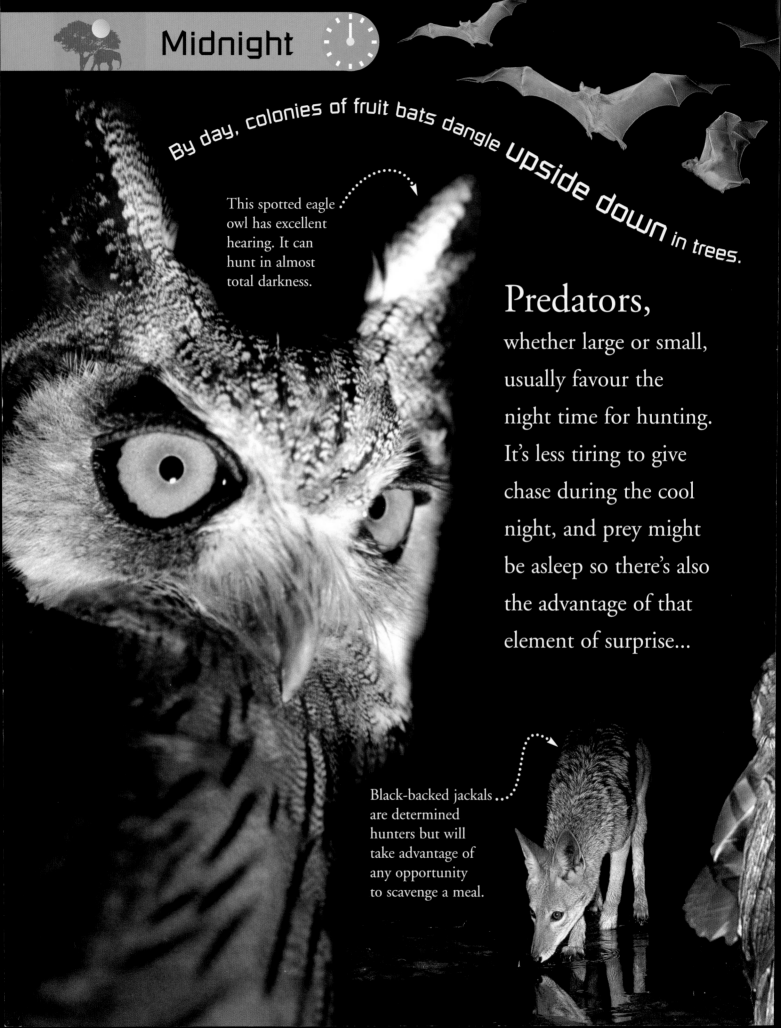

By day, colonies of fruit bats dangle upside down in trees.

This spotted eagle owl has excellent hearing. It can hunt in almost total darkness.

Predators,

whether large or small, usually favour the night time for hunting. It's less tiring to give chase during the cool night, and prey might be asleep so there's also the advantage of that element of surprise...

Black-backed jackals are determined hunters but will take advantage of any opportunity to scavenge a meal.

At night, they **swarm out** squeaking and whistling in search of fruit to eat.

Owls see well by day and night, but they have to swivel their heads because they can't move their eyeballs.

An unfortunate mouse barely has time to realize what's happening. This barn owl suddenly and silently grabs and kills it, swallowing it whole – fur, bones, and all. In a few hours time the owl will produce a pellet from its mouth containing the bits it has been unable to digest.

Nightjars feed on insects, literally grabbing them as they fly by.

43

Black rhinos have little eyes and poor eyesight but very sensitive hearing and smell. They tend to spend the day resting in the shade and feed at night. When two meet each other at a water hole they huff and snort, kick up the dust, and then generally ignore each other.

Lions sometimes attack small, adolescent black rhinos, but they don't usually go for adults like this one.

There's just not enough vegetation available to support many black rhinos so each animal lives alone, marking out its territory with urine and dung to keep others away. A pair of rhinos are usually a mating couple who will stay together for a few days, or a mother and her calf.

Giraffes and elephants are often at the water hole in the middle of the night. They sleep far less than humans – about five hours out of 24 – and spend almost all of their waking hours eating. Elephants are particularly frequent visitors as they need to drink as much as 200 litres (53 gallons) a day.

The hooked lip of the black rhino is useful for pulling leafy branches into its mouth.

From dawn to dusk

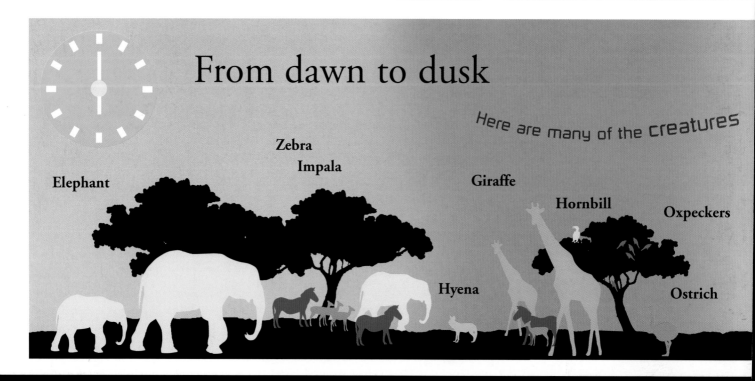

Here are many of the creatures

Elephant Zebra Impala Giraffe Hornbill Oxpeckers Hyena Ostrich

Glossary

Here are the meanings of some of the important words you will come across as you learn about the animals and birds that visit the water hole.

ADOLESCENT An animal that is no longer a baby, but isn't yet a fully-grown adult capable of mating.

BACHELOR A male animal that does not have a female to mate with during the mating season.

BURROW A hole in the ground dug by animals so that they can live or hide in it.

CARCASS The dead body of an animal.

DUNG The waste matter produced by an animal.

EXOSKELETON The hard covering that some animals and insects have outside their bodies.

FLOCK A group of birds that live and fly together.

GRAZE To feed on grass or other green plants.

GROOMING The way that animals keep their fur and skin clean and free of insects.

HERD A group of animals, such as zebra or kudu.

INSECT REPELLENT A substance whose smell or taste keeps insects away.

MATING The way in which a male and a female animal come together to produce young.

MOB A group of meerkats.

PACK The name for a group of jackals or hyenas that live together.

PELLET A ball of bones and feathers spat out by an owl some time after swallowing its prey.

PREDATOR The name for an animal that hunts, kills, and eats other animals.

PREY The animal that a predator hunts, kills, and eats.

PRIDE The name for a group of lions that live together.

REGURGITATE To bring food back out of the stomach to chew it again or feed it to someone else.

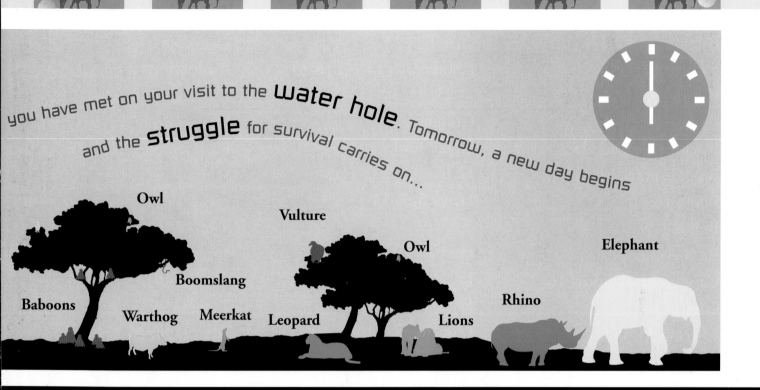

you have met on your visit to the **water hole**. Tomorrow, a new day begins and the **struggle** for survival carries on...

Owl

Vulture

Owl

Elephant

Boomslang

Baboons

Rhino

Warthog   Meerkat   Leopard   Lions

RODENT Animals such as squirrels or beavers that have strong teeth for chewing.

SCAVENGER An animal that eats dead animals but doesn't kill them itself.

SENTRIES Guards who warn the rest of the pack that danger is approaching.

SPARRING Playful fighting between young male giraffes that doesn't aim to cause actual injury.

STALKING To follow an animal silently in order to launch a surprise attack.

VENOM The poison that scorpions and snakes inject into their attackers by biting or stinging.

Picture credits

The publisher would like to thank the following for their kind permission to reproduce their photographs:
(Key: a-above; c-centre; b-below; l-left; r-right; t-top)

Alamy Images: David Wall 26tl; Martin Harvey 37tl, 37tr; **Steve Bloom Images** 2tl, 2-3b, 3tc, 3tr, 3tr, 4tl, 6tl, 6-7, 8cb, 8-9c, 8l, 10-11, 12tl, 15br, 29tl, 32tl, 32-33, 33br, 40tl, 40, 41cl, 41cr, 41br, 45tl. **Ardea.com:** Chris Harvey 13crb; Clem Haagner 28br, 29bl, 39br; Joanna Van Gruisen 11br; Peter Steyn 7crb. **Bruce Coleman Ltd:** Carol Hughes 11crb; Christer Fredriksson 35r; John Shaw 45b. **Corbis:** Clem Haagner/Gallo Images 17crb; Darrell Gulin 33cr; David A. Northcott 42tr, 42-43t; Gallo Images 17tr, 18l, 37cla, 37cl, 37clb; Gavin G. Thomson/Gallo Images 21tr; George McCarthy 43b; Hein von Horsten/Gallo Images 43r; Jeffrey L. Rotman 38-39b; Joe McDonald 26bl; Lynda Richardson 13cra; Marcello Calandrini 7cr; Martin Harvey 7br, 23cra; Martin Harvey/Gallo Images 7tr, 36bl, 36-37cb; Mary Ann McDonald 9cr, 12bl; Nigel J. Dennis/Gallo Images 20tl, 20br, 27tl, 27tr; Paul A. Souders 9tr; Peter Johnson 24cl, 25tr, 29br, 42br, 43bl; Richard du Toit/Gallo Images 28tl; Rick Doyle 19cr; Roger De La Harpe/Gallo Images 24-25c; Roger Tidman 15crb, 41crb; Ron Sanford 13cr; Steve Bein 21bl; Tim Davis 9cra; Tom Brakefield 11tr;

William Manning 23cra; Winifred Wisniewski/Frank Lane Picture Agency 21b; Wolfgang Kaehler 18br, 19bl, 19br, 20bl; Yann Arthus-Bertrand 23tr. **DK Images:** Jerry Young 16tl, 27crb; Philip Dowell 34clb. **FLPA - images of nature:** Frans Lanting/Minden Pictures 1; Michael & Patricia Fogden/Minden Pictures 7cra; William S. Clark 23crb. **Getty Images:** Blake Little 44b; Darrell Gulin 25b; Daryl Balfour 9cb; Gallo Images/Heinrich van den Berg 3tc, 23br, 32bl; Gallo Images/Daryl Balfour 24b; James Balog 33tr; Jonathan & Angela 13tr; Jonathan & Angela Scott 37br; Peter Lilja 15tr; Stuart Westmorland 41cra. **N.H.P.A.:** Jonathan & Angela Scott 38l. **National Geographic Image Collection:** Chris Johns 30l, 33cra, 34-35b; Kim Wolhuter 39tl, 42bl; Mattias Klum 30-31bc, 31br; Volkmar K.Wentzel 28bl. **Nature Picture Library Ltd:** Bruce Davidson 5cra, 5cr; Herman Brehm 11cra; Peter Blackwell 41tr; Richard du Toit 12-13, 27br, 29crb, 35cl; Ron O'Connor 39crb; Sharon Heald 29cra, 39cr; Terry Andrewartha 15cr; Tony Heald 48. **OSF/photolibrary.com:** Alan Hartley 33crb; Michael Fogden 3tl, 22tl, 22-23; Osolinski Stan 16-17c. **Wynand & Claudia du Plessis:** 2tr, 14tl, 14-15. Roberta Stacey: 31tl. **Still Pictures:** Heike Fischer 16bl; Martin Harvey 17cra. Additional photography Ginger Mauney. All other images © Dorling Kindersley www.dkimages.com